Design My Fresh

A Sneaker Design Book

Printed in the United States of America

9781674965055

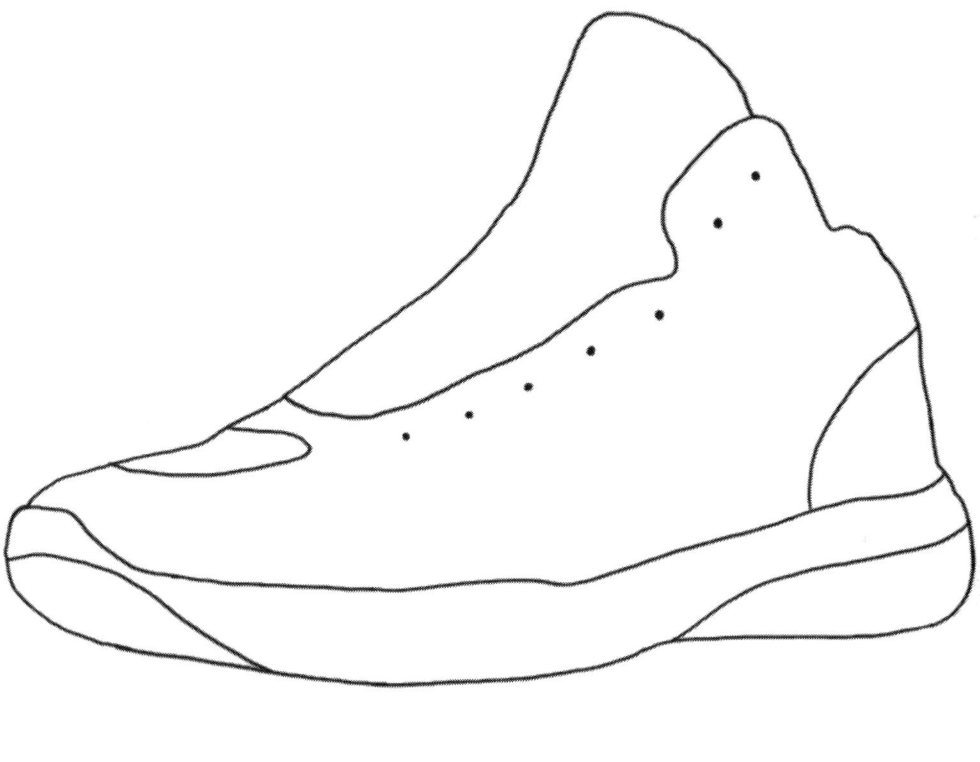

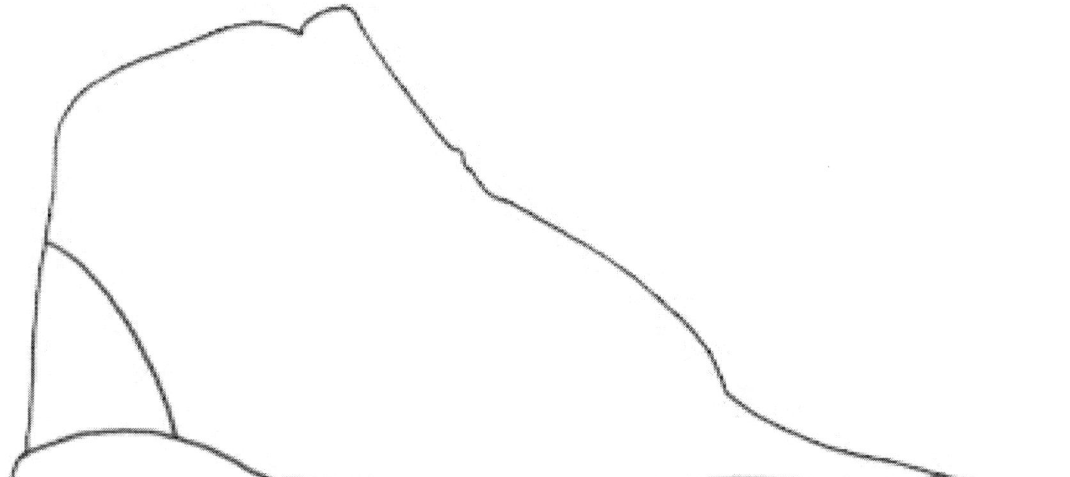

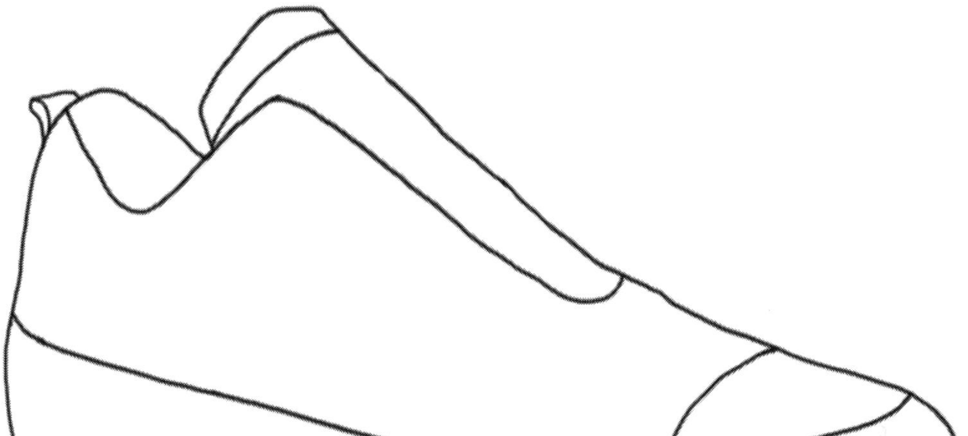

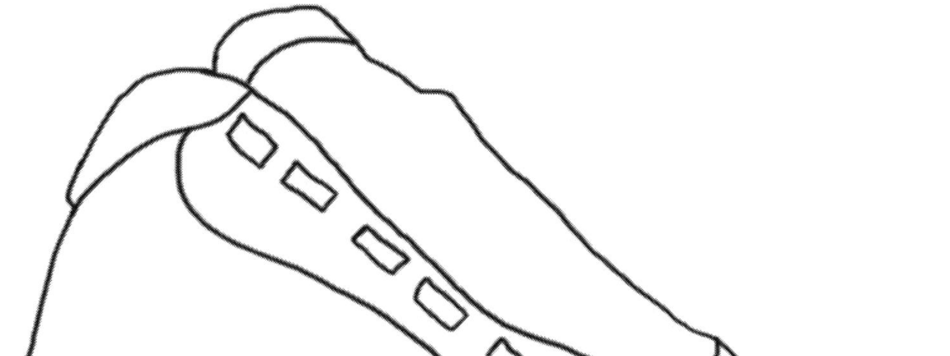

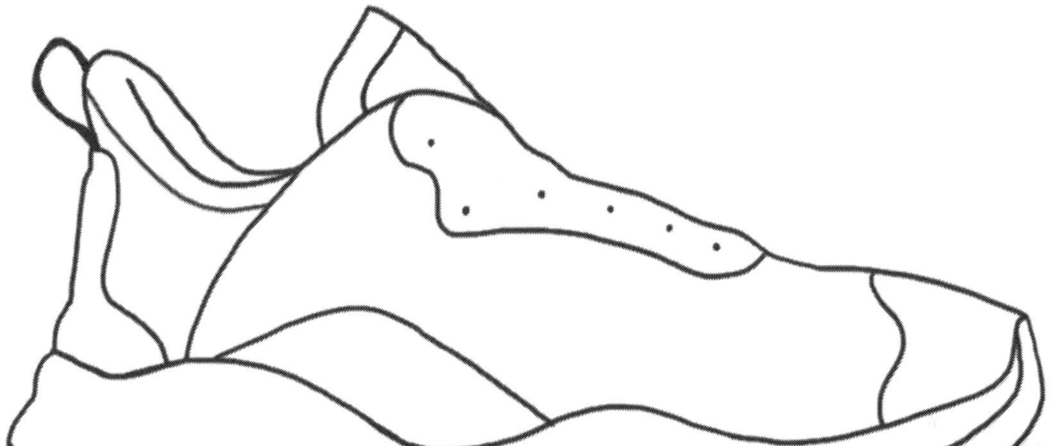

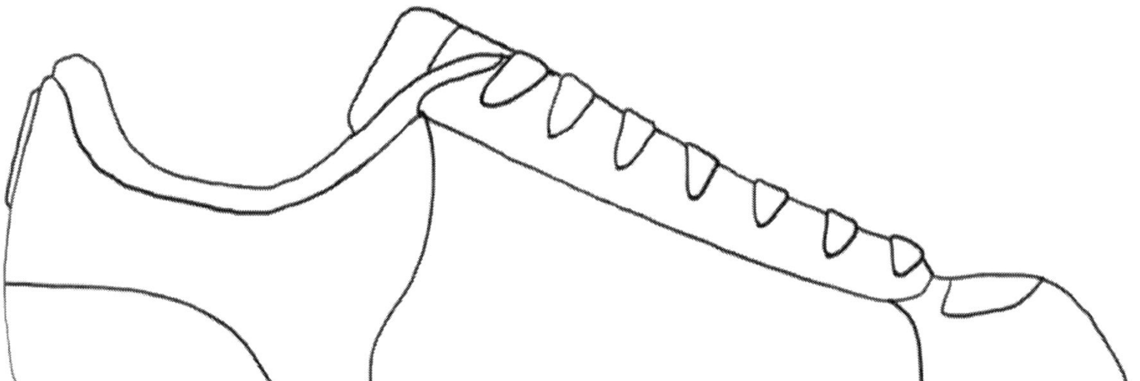

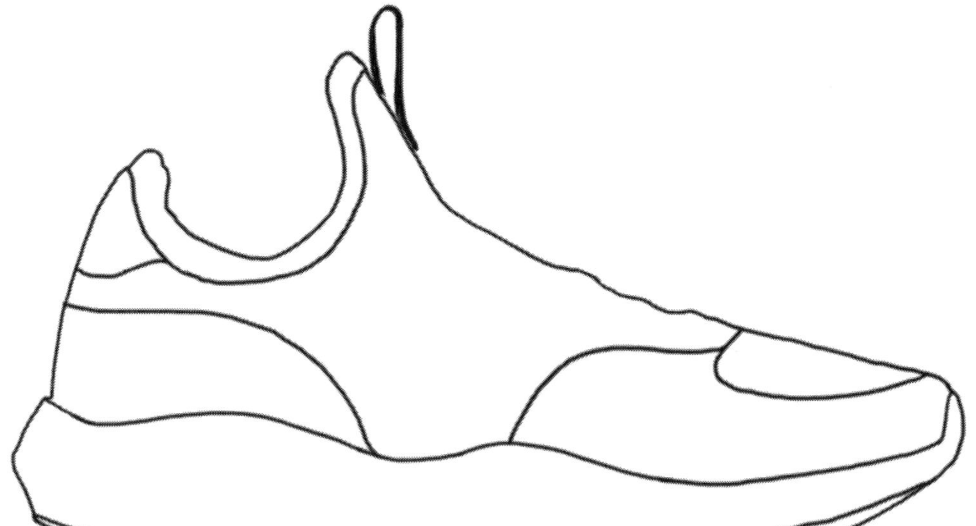

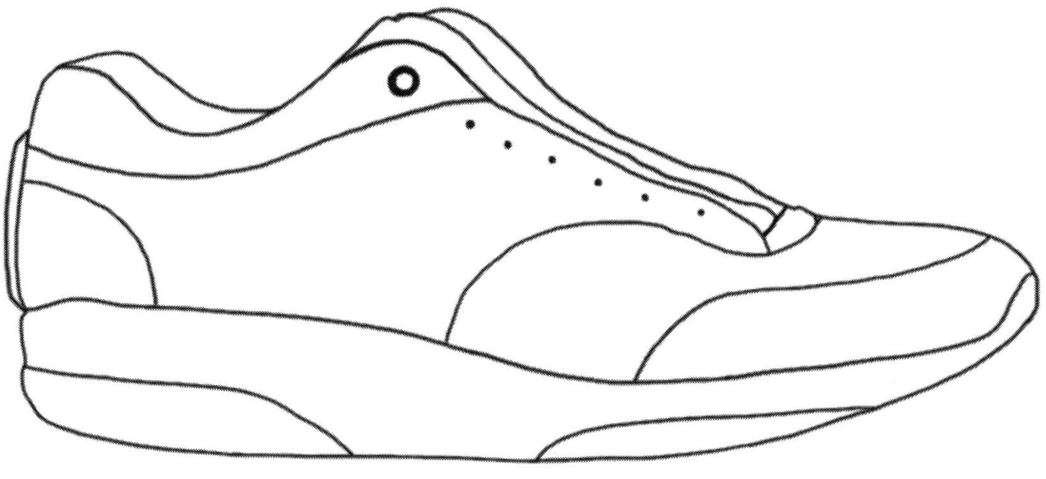

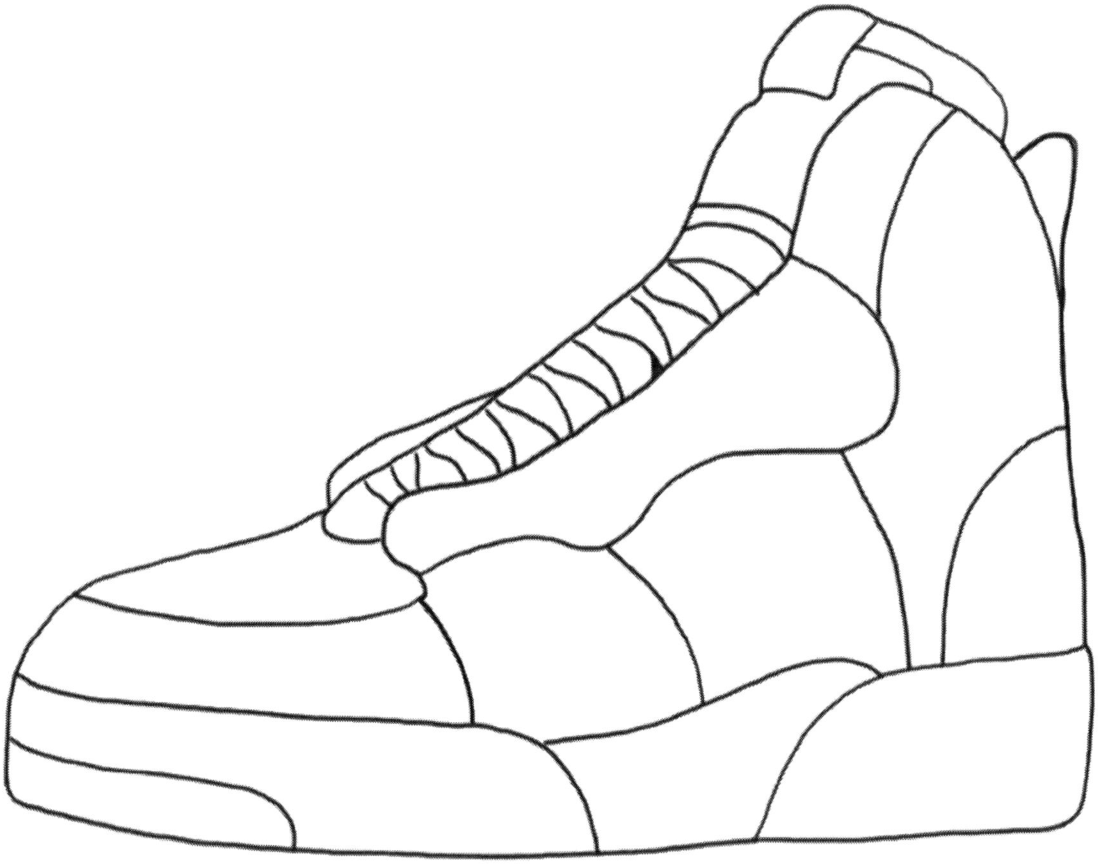

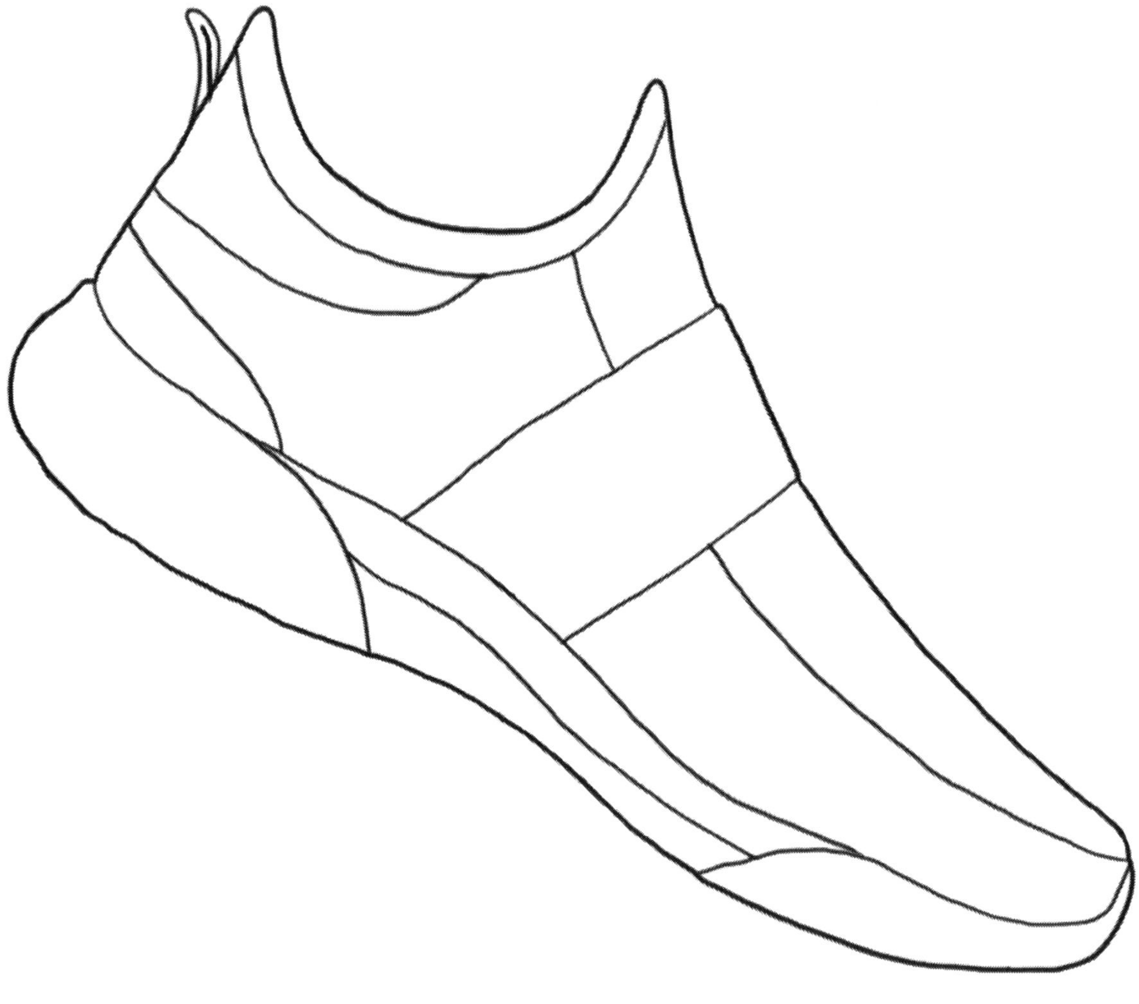

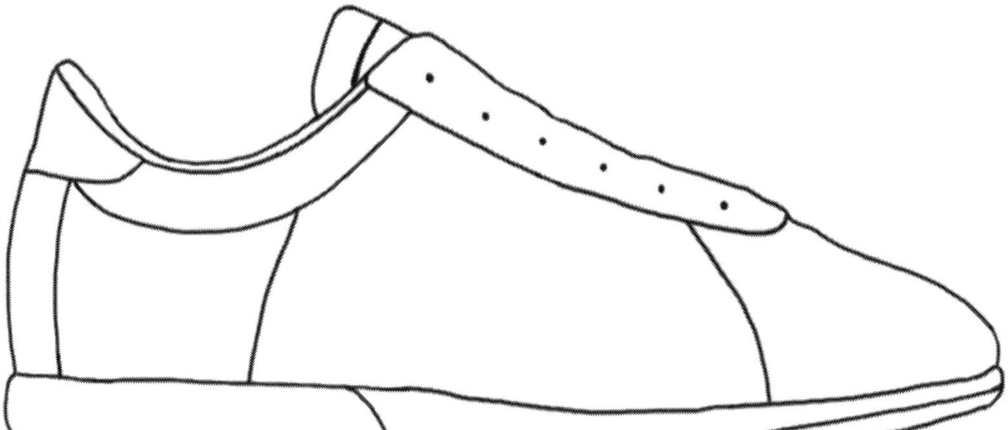

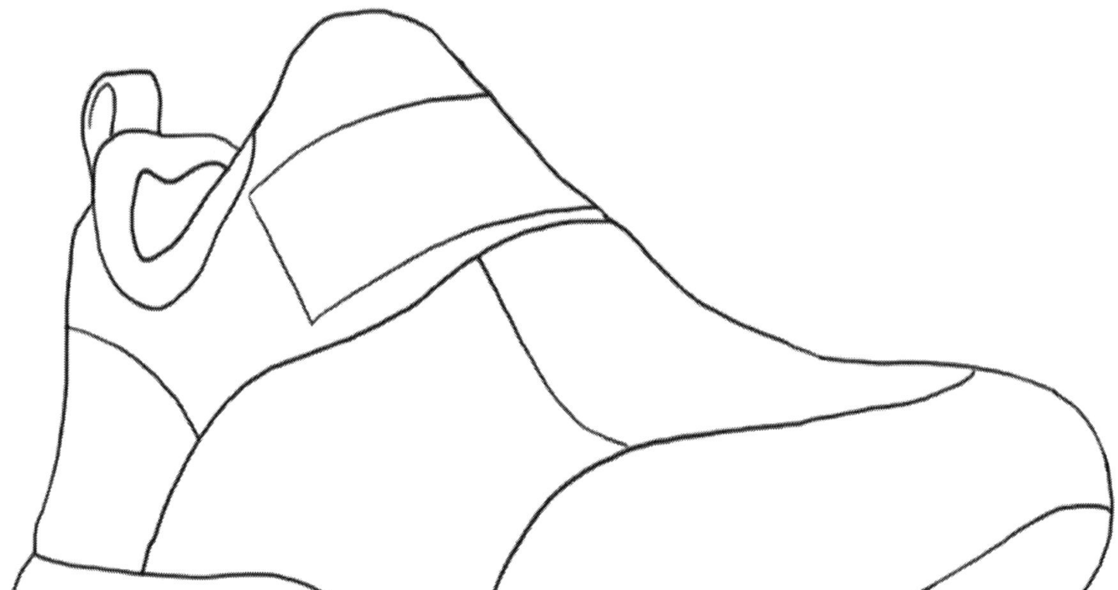

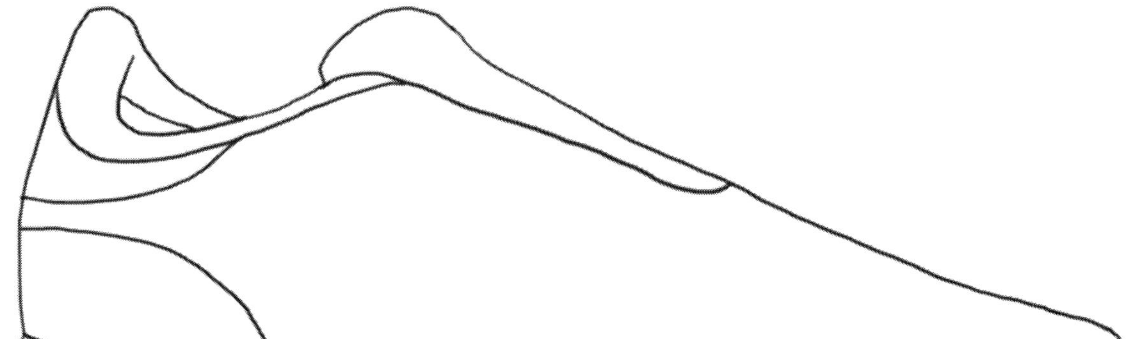

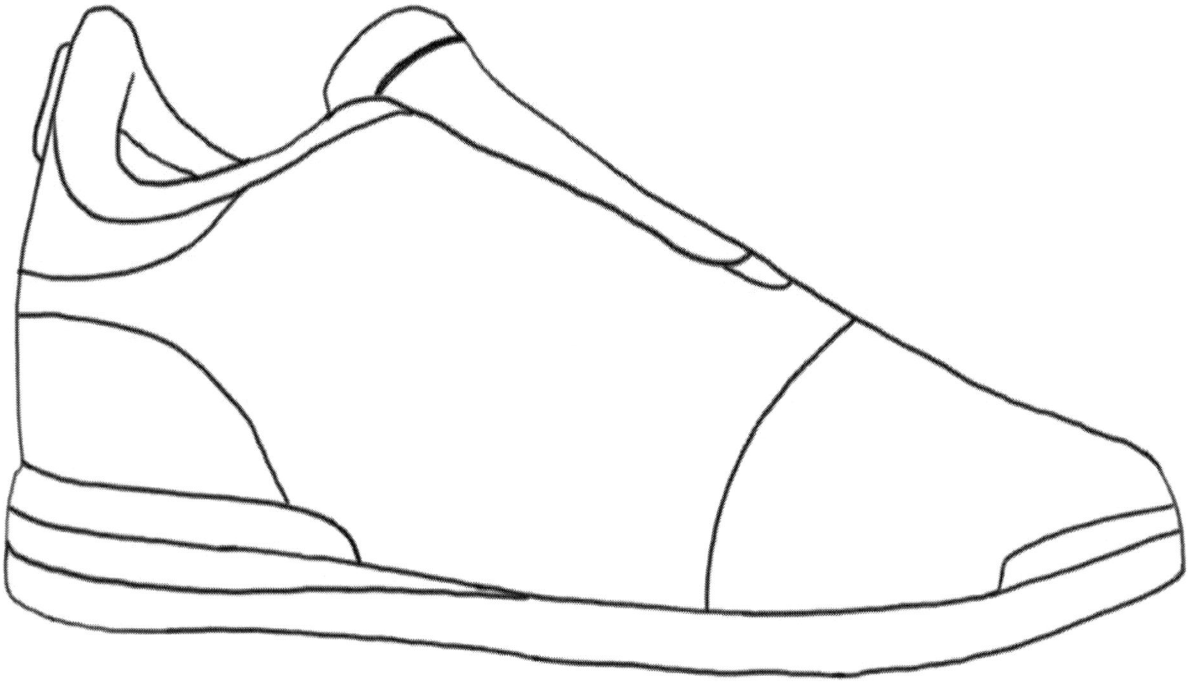

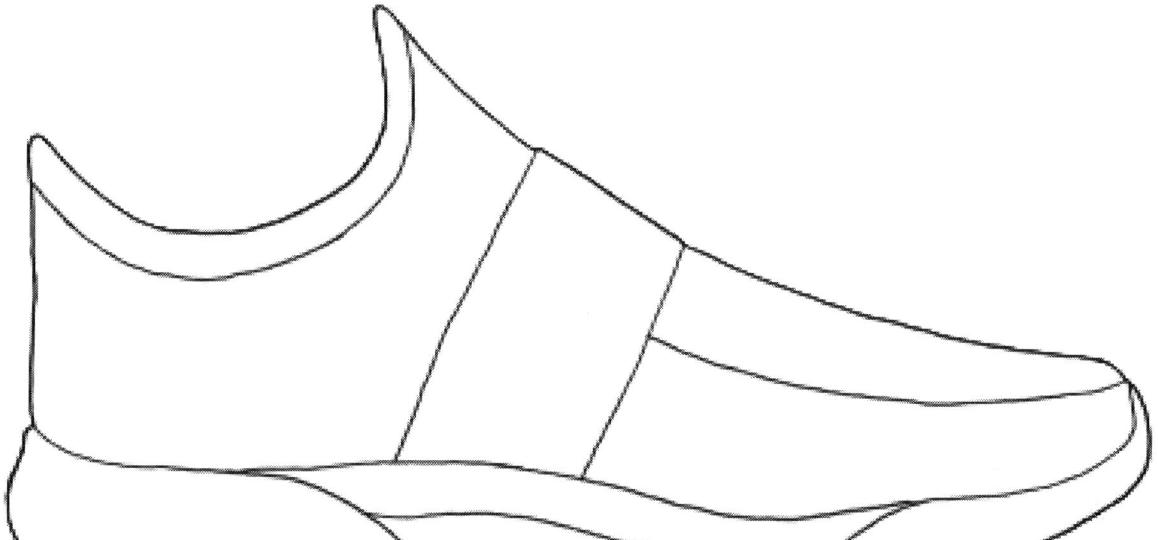

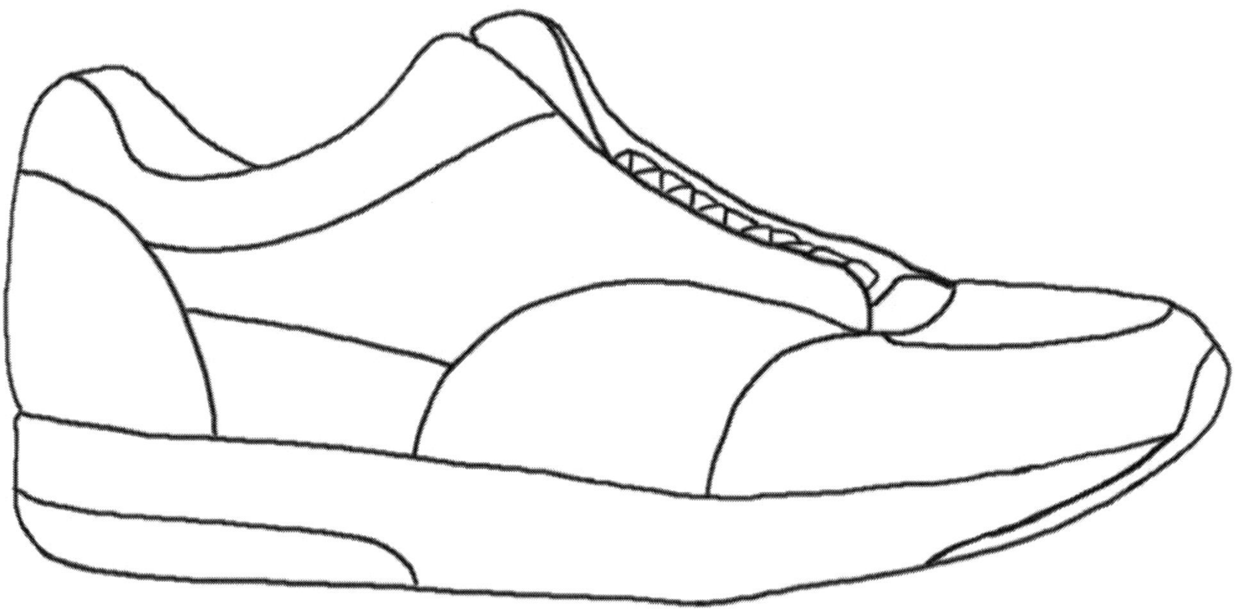

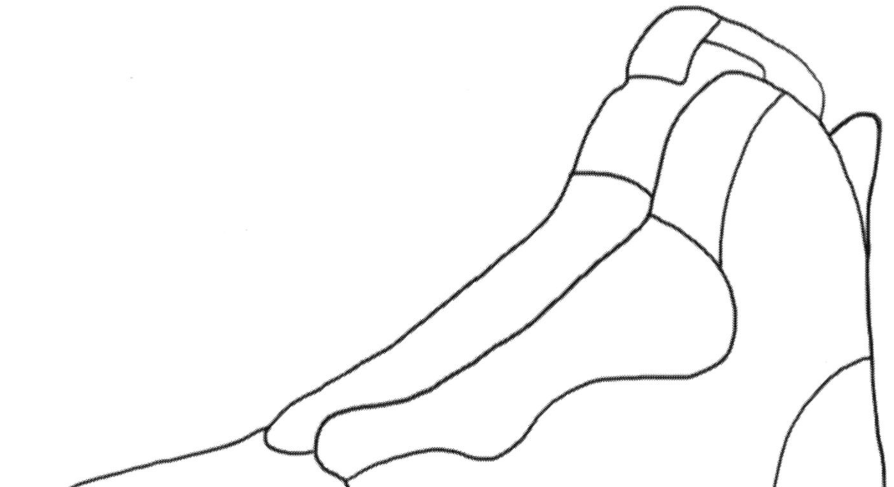

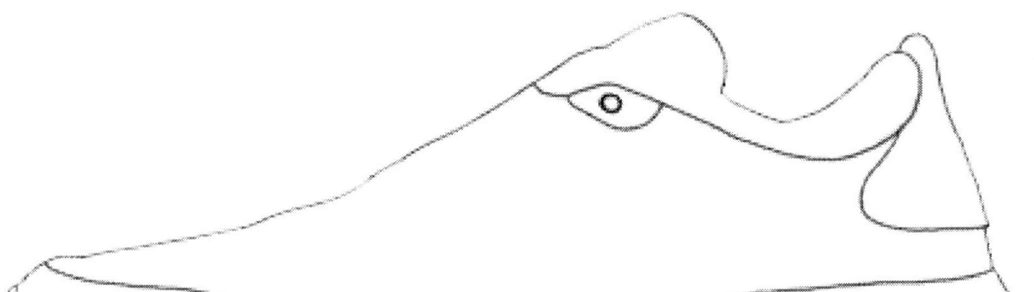

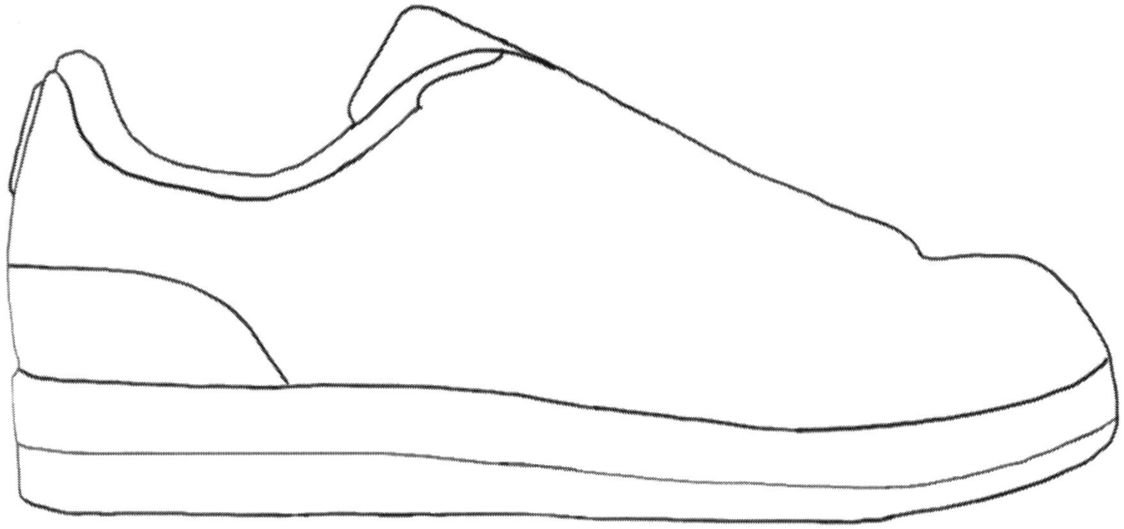

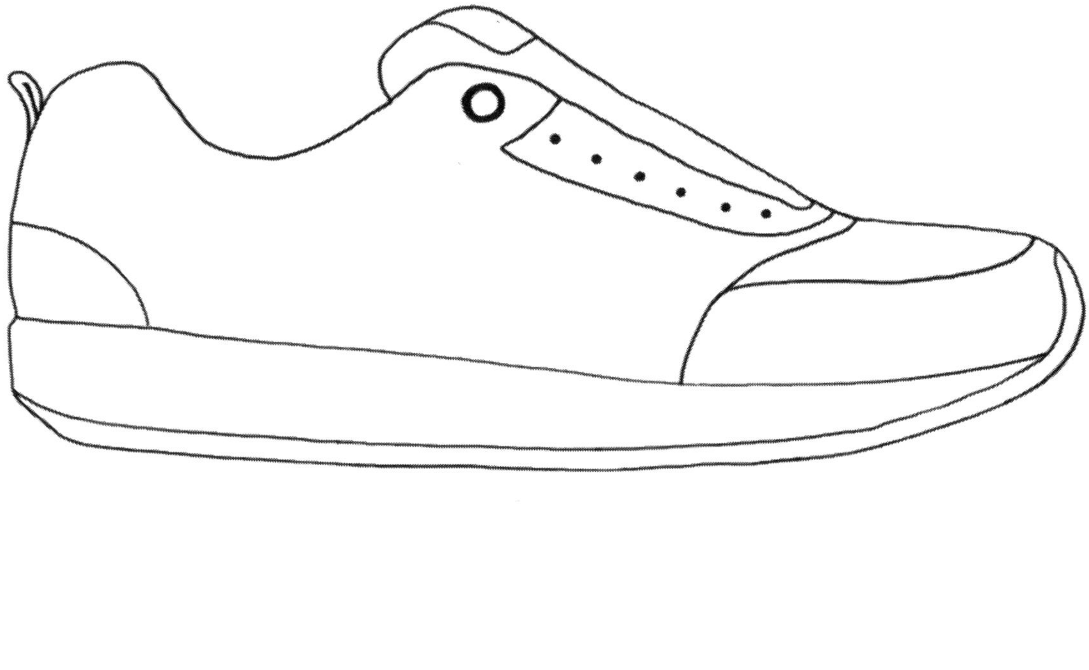

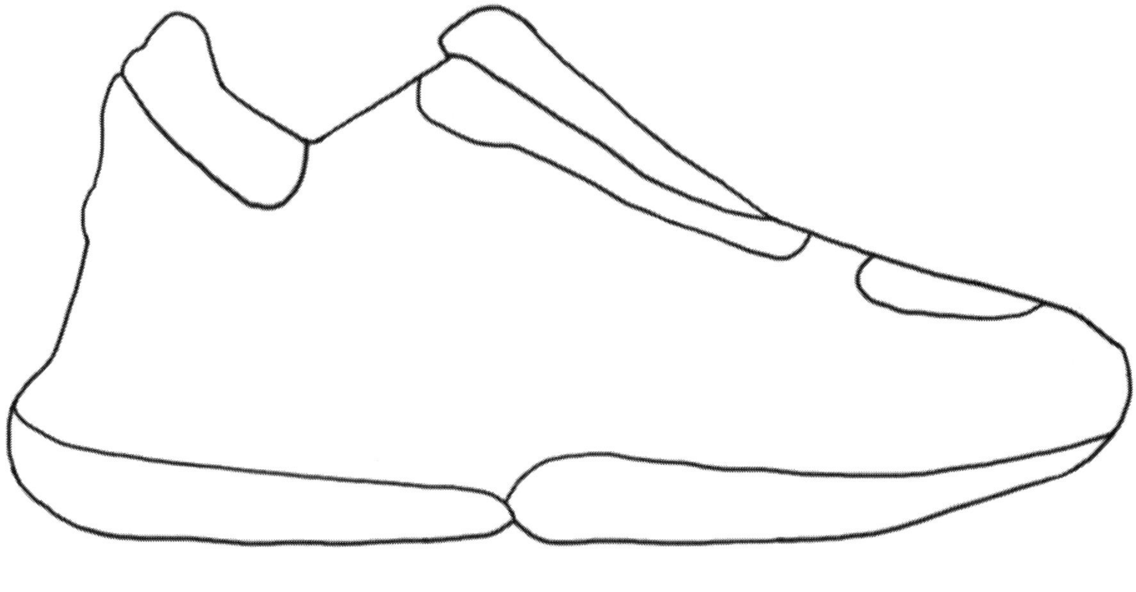

Made in United States
Troutdale, OR
12/12/2024

26377951R00029